NEW TOWNS

An Anthology of Place Writing

Wild Pressed Books

First Edition

ISBN 978-1-9163774-0-0

NEW TOWNS ©2020 by Wild Pressed Books.
Copyright for individual works remains with the authors.

Cover Design by Tracey Scott-Townsend

Published by Wild Pressed Books: 2020
Wild Pressed Books, UK Business Reg. No. 09550738
http://www.wildpressedbooks.com
All Rights Reserved.

No part of this publication may be reproduced or transmitted in any form by any means electronic, mechanical, photocopying, recording or otherwise, without the prior permission of the copyright owner.

The publisher has no control over, and is not responsible for, any third party websites or their contents.

NEW TOWNS

Introduction

This collection of writing is a unique creative exploration of the genius loci and sense of place found in New Towns across the UK. We're defining *New Towns* by those associated with the New Towns Act 1946, and the subsequent waves of development following the Second World War: the waves of 1946, 1961-64 and 1967-70. These towns were designed to alleviate housing shortages by expanding into the UK's Green Belt and areas considered "overspill" close to large cities.

That said, some already existing conurbations were designated with New Town status during these waves, this included town planning and housing projects in keeping with the design and ethos of the wider projects. For obvious reasons we've been unable to creatively capture every New Town on the map, and in some instances the pieces here have a more general feel about New-Town-ness. What this anthology is, however, is a glimpse at a handful of sites that all share similar histories, social and cultural make-up, and founding principles.

New Towns were conceived of with a utopian ideal in mind; focusing on a natural, neighbourly, suburban way of life – one that allowed its residents escape from the toxic environment of urban life, reverting back to a pre-industrial aesthetic and ethos. Every type of home for every type of individual and family were built – often in sites and directions to maximise fresh air and sunshine. We might see it as a precursor to current ecological campaigns. As many of the works in this book confirm, the landscape in these texts offer forms of escape, respite and refuge.

Every district were to have easy access to good schools and nurseries, play areas and parks. Every district were to have their own shopping districts, churches and community centres. This too is recorded in these pieces; where the regions' functionality opens up latitudes of civil ease and unease. The New Town was designed to be a cultural centre too, where its civic centre had a theatre, cinema and concert hall; although much of the writing here, considers the cultural lack, especially in terms of formative teenage experience.

In subsequent years and decades, this vision has not fulfilled its promises. Towns like Telford, Milton Keynes, Derry or Cwmbran have been left in the cultural and socio-economic shadow of their urban big brothers and rural little sisters. The infrastructures have aged and the small, stretched councils lack the funding and capacity to revitalise them. They're seen as lacking the cultural capital that comes with historic towns or vibrant cities, and are often marginalised as "Service Station" type regions with little to offer outside of convenient commuting distances. The creative writers showcased here explore New Towns in these limbo positions. These are almost-places. Not-quite towns. And are now no-longer-new.

There is something eerie and haunting about these places – areas that promised release and relief, and still show the slightly faded signs of these promises. Towns that glimpsed at a possible future, but are caught in the defunct eddy of that glance. Some offer another distinctly uncanny feel too – places like Ravenscraig in Scotland, or Poundbury in England hold a special kind of unfinished modernity, a 'too new to be real' spirit that some have called 'Grimly Cute'. Perhaps why this anthology has yielded so many characters that are "on their marks". They are about to arrive, about to return, about to become something else.

The UK literary world is riding a wave of great place-writing at the moment. From the New Nature Writers like Robert McFarlane and Helen McDonald to writers like Paul Farley who rethink the postindustrial edges of our estates. From projects like Places of Poetry to the digital site-specific work of Birmingham's Overhear and Hull's QR Poetry. Writers have investigated coasts and rivers, hamlet and city, wild and tamed. This is the first creative anthology with singular attention to these important yet overlooked areas of the UK landscape, featuring writers from and who deal with these uniquely haunting places.

In these pages you'll find an array of perspectives and styles; from personal essay to short story, concrete poem to monologue. What they share is a focus on the disparate elements that make up place-identity in these places. There is a focus on outsider views from subcultures; as if the labyrinthine roadways and in-between economic and social status of these towns give rise to voices that are finding themselves and figuring themselves out, through contrasts and clashes in their surroundings. The poetic voices in this collection are both arriving and static, getting out and incapable of escaping. But this is not without tenderness. The poetry and prose on display here recognise the peculiar and overlooked beauty of these spaces - they say, we not just overspills and tagged-on parts of wider conurbations; they ask, importantly, how long do we have to be here until we're no longer still just "new".

I'm thrilled to be the editor of this important book and thank all contributors for their wonderful work.

R.M. Francis

R. M. Francis is a lecturer in Creative and Professional Writing at the University of Wolverhampton. His novel, Bella, was published with Wild Pressed Books, who are also publishing his collection of Flash Fictions, The Wrenna, in 2021. He has published five poetry pamphlets and his collection of poems, Subsidence, is due out with Smokestack Books in December 2020. He was the inaugural David Bradshaw writer in Residence at the University of Oxford and is currently poet in residence for the Black Country Geological Society.

List of Authors and their Work

Helen Angell   Apollo Landing

Craig Austin   Crow Valley Particulars

Jane Burn   The Apollo Pavillion

Brian Comber   From a Ford Zephyr

Steve Corton   In Basildon Plaza

Sarah Davy   Hiding Place

Murdo Eason   I Remember Glenrothes

Harry Gallagher   New Town Old Story
                          Bracknell

Mark Goodwin   A Gap, A Construct, An English Edge

Steve Harrison   Dawley New Town
                          Rabbit Run

Sarah James   While Visiting
                          Orbiting Redditch

Alison Jones   Overspill

Richard Lakin   Tribes, Tech and Take Me Home

Laurence Mitchell   An Embarrassment of Roundabouts

Heather Moulson   Harlow, 1971

Marcelle Newbold   Map of Llandarcy

Nick Pearson   The Roundabouts of Telford
                          Last Exit to Telford

Finola Scott   Cumbernauld New Town

Billy Stanton   Screwfix

Rob Walton   Galleries Washington
                          Geocaching

Kim Whysall-Hammond   Glimpse
                          Winter in Concrete

Contents

	Page
The Apollo Pavillion	1
Hiding Place	3
Orbiting Redditch	8
I Remember Glenrothes (After Perec and Brainard)	9
Last Exit to Telford	18
Crow Valley Particulars	19
Bracknell	29
An Embarrassment of Roundabouts – Redditch New Town	30
Galleries, Washington	38
Apollo Landing	39
While Visiting	41
Overspill	43
Harlow 1971	46
From a Ford Zephyr six	48
Rabbit Run	50
Map of Llandarcy / Coed Darcy 2008	51
Screwfix	52
The Roundabouts of Telford	57
Glimpse	58
Cumbernauld	59
Dawley New Town 1963-8	61
New Town, Old Story	62
Tribes, Tech and Take Me Home – Telford is 50	63
A Gap, a Construct Town, an English Edge	68

In Basildon Plaza 69
Geocaching 70
Winter in concrete 71

The Apollo Pavillion[1]

was a Tomorrow's idea of alien worlds. It watches the lines
of its own quadratic face reflected in the man-made lake,

lawns around it sculpting an imagined movie set,
like a dream of distant planets.
Stout square legs moor this flight of abstracts

to the Earth. This centrepiece of Sunny Blunts Estate
was built to speak a language of futures,
to blot the history of slums,
to gather up the sprawl of colliery folk
and offer them the sight of its space-age skin,
its bold blocks of bright and shade,

its daubed haunt of biomorph ghosts,
its ambitious interplay of shadowed sun.
This was optimism – this was no bucolic place
but a Brutalist view, a modernist seed, sown upon memories
of slag and smoke. The geometry of cubes holds its corners

of cruel wind, cuts itself into angles of dusk.
It wonders if it failed.
Concrete spalling, piss-stained corridors scuzzed with weed,

whitewash grimed with slicks of distopian green,
it was left to rot in its own ideals.
It still feels the scar where someone once sprayed

a vision of their own – LIFE IS CHEAP DEATH IS FREE.
Nobody's utopia. Google tells you *Marmite, folly, eyesore,
   grubby.*

---

[1]A famous and controversial landmark in Peterlee, County Durham, the Apollo Pavilion was built in 1969. It was designed by Victor Pasmore, Consulting Director of Urban Design of Peterlee's New Town Development Corporation (1955-1970's). It fell into disrepair after much vandalism and there were calls to pull it down. Thankfully it was saved and restored in 2019. Peterlee was founded in 1948 as part of the New Town Act and as a result of the document *Farewell Squalor: a Design for a New Town and Proposals for the Re-Development of the Easington Rural District, 1946.*

Me, I'm glad it was saved. I love this curious dream,
its trick of seeing the north through vacant squares.
There can be no *Farewell Squalor* in the end,
no blotting out of the poor, no building us out of the way.
No magic wand because the haves still have and the nots do
    not.

Jane Burn

Hiding Place

I'm eating beans cold from the tin when Mum tells me to pack my bag and we run. My hair is still wet from the bath and I'm wearing most of my clothes so we don't have to carry them. We hold hands on the bus and I try to reach the dried sauce on my chin with my tongue. Streets race by and house after house turns to sodden field then slick wet motorway for hours. I wonder when we'll go back for my Mega Drive.

'The office won't be open until morning,' Mum says when we reach the last stop.

She takes us to a dark corner of the bus station and puts her coat over me. I don't sleep and neither does the city, turning people over from work to pubs then home in fogs and rages of drink and vomit. A man cleans chewing gum off the floor and seats with a scraper, working around the bin bags at our feet. As soon as the sun comes up, we go. Mum bangs on the office door until a light flicks through the cracked glass and it swings open.

'I know it's a while since I rang but you said we could come. It just took a while to get sorted. So here we are,' The words fall out of Mum in one long breath. The lady at the door smiles.

We get a room on the second floor. When I see babies in the mouldy shared kitchen, I think their screaming will ruin my sleep, but I'm wrong. At night women cry and cry. A little girl soils herself and her Mum uses the communal shower to rinse out the clothes, but the plughole gets blocked. The floor never feels clean, so I wash at the sink and foam the soap, imagine I'm in a hot bath full of bubbles until Mum shouts me back because I've overdone our turn.

Our room has no window and is stuffy at night. Mum lies next to me, lets me rest my head on the rise and fall of her chest until I fall asleep. Her tummy is swelling and she can't sleep for it, her fingers tracing the shape over and over until it kicks. It won't be long until there are three of us.

I count 23 days in the narrow room on two hard beds until we're moving again. The lady we met on our first day lets me take the Subbuteo mat from the sitting room. 'No-one else has ever bothered with it and you'll need something to make your new room yours'.

She rolls it up, wedges it into my backpack and drops a handful of players and balls in the inside pocket. All our things are in blue and red checked bags and I've got new trainers that light up as we walk down the street to the bus stop. Mum turns to say something when the lady waves us off but can't so I shout, 'Thank you, thank you, thank you,' until it bounces off the doors and windows.

Mum checks the hand-drawn map with instructions she was given with a set of keys and we change buses once. The second takes us from the edge of town and winds like thread over and under a straight grey road. Signs with numbers and no place names point off to roundabouts covered in grass and stumps of new trees. I wonder how we'll find our way back if we have to run again.

'Won't be long,' Mum pats my knee.

'Will I go to a new school?' It's been bothering me since we left.

'Not yet. After the summer holidays. Gives us plenty of time to settle in. Look, it's our stop.'

The driver stops and waves to us and in a moment we're off, standing with our bags on the threshold of somewhere completely new. Mum's hand is cool, not clammy, when I squeeze it. This is good.

The new house is all ours. It has three floors and a downstairs toilet and Mum can't stop talking about it.

'Look at this light! On, off, on off. It's like a film!' She looks at herself in the illuminated mirror, her careful smile wider now. The cut on her chin is healed but she'll always have a scar.

My room is on the top floor, the whole loft with a ceiling too high to touch and a cool glass window that lets me look up to blue July sky or over red tiled roofs and tidy lawns. Trees make a fence around the gardens. I can't see over and could be anywhere. I've rolled out the Subbuteo mat and lost a ball between a gap in the floorboards already. Mum is on the top step, leaning her head against the wall, light falling over her face.

'We'll get you a nice carpet when the family allowance comes through. Come here'. She pushes a coin into my hand, brushes my cheek. 'Go and explore. We need a nap'. Her hand cradles her tummy and I help her stand and navigate the narrow stairs.

The shop is round the corner next to a takeaway and a pub on a three-sided square that is perfect when you stand back and look at it. There's a clock right in the middle high up and I like the way the shrubs sit neatly in brick walls and the smooth concrete balls that line the edges. There was no green near the old house. I buy a Caramac and perch on the wall. A boy with a limp and a broken arm comes out of the shop and sits next to me.

'I'm Chris' he says. 'I got run over. Do you wanna sign me cast?'

I have to listen hard as his words come out fast. At first, I can't understand everything he says. Like Mam instead of Mum and ganning instead of going. Both floundering in the space between summer and school, we agree to meet every day in the same spot. Chris brings big bags of Discos and felt tip pens. We draw pictures on his cast and I try not to look at the raw stapled scar on his scalp or the lonely tuft of hair where they shaved it to open him up and save him. His Mam blames this place, its winding roads with no white lines and cobbled paths and one-way bus lanes. Chris shows me the clipping from the paper, his Mam stern with folded arms, his Dad pointing at the road.

'Look, they say much-loved local schoolboy. Everyone knows me now. No-one even shouts fatty anymore and Mam lets me eat whatever I want'.

One day we walk, slowly with Chris's limp. He isn't allowed to cross the main road so we have to stick to paths. No matter which way we go, we end up in a close, all red brick houses and lawns and angles and empty parking spaces. Every fourth house is painted white, a strange sore thumb that makes everything harder to tell apart. We have to turn around and go back. To the centre, the square, the chiming clock and the tidy leaves so green they hardly seem real.

'I hate it here,' says Chris. 'Always going round in circles, like a puzzle you can't get out of. When I'm old enough, I'm off'.

I don't tell him, but I plan on staying, if I can. I feel wrapped tight in those same circles, in symmetry and quarter hour chimes. I live on Caradoc Close, not a long spine of a street full of raised voices and sirens and questions in the night. I feel safe when I walk home and see the same faces, know that anyone from outside will be noticed and let known they're not welcome. I hear Mum lock the door and check it twice. I practice writing my new name, so I don't slip up when I go back to school.

We meet every day until the holidays. Chris is going to Cornwall for the summer, to a house near a beach with a swimming pool and a tennis court. Me and Mam are painting the little room ready for the baby, my new brother or sister. I'm saving half my pocket money to buy a teddy for the cot. We watch the bus crawl up the one-way road over the new speed bump that Chris has named after himself. A sea of maroon and black blazers pile off and go into the shop three at a time. Then I see Mum waving. She's been to the big Asda and has a full bag and a full heart and I'm finally able to let out my breath and feel like we're home.

Sarah Davy

Orbiting Redditch

The town boasts
a large shopping mall,

identical box houses and   On the map, it's the scab
the nearest hospital.   of a scratched itch, healed
                             over.

In the car, it's a circling   in curves of grounded grey,
of tarmac, a looping the loop   longing for clear direction.

Lost somewhere within this,
I'm searching for signs –

even a splash of red   Half an hour late now, I try
would suggest life.   to follow the neon blue

of a flashing siren,   When I finally get there, I slot
and avoid all the ditches.   my car into a small grey
                             space.

Inside, I wait for the doctor,
who's still not arrived yet.

Sarah James

I Remember Glenrothes (After Perec and Brainard)

> *How long*
> *Do works endure? As long*
> *As they are not completed.*
> *Since as long as they demand effort*
> *They do not decay.*
> (Bertolt Brecht)

I remember we lived for a short time in Victoria Avenue, Milnathort, whilst we waited for our new house, in Glenrothes, to be 'finished'.

I remember moving from Milnathort to Glenrothes. The removal van broke down beside the Orwell standing stones, just outside Kinross.

I remember our first house in Clyde Court, Rimbleton precinct. All the precincts (housing schemes) in Glenrothes were named after the old farms on which mass housing was subsequently built. Rimbleton streets were named after Scottish rivers, estuaries and sea lochs such as: Clyde Court, Tay Court, Lorne Court, Laxford Road and Moray Place.

I remember pre-school years of rivers and hills. Running through the pavement tributaries of our estuarial precinct and whenever you looked through the vennels to the North, you could see another world beyond the periphery of the town. No buildings, but instead, fields and trees expanding towards a horizon punctuated by the rounded contours of the Twa Paps o' Fife: East Lomond and West Lomond.

I remember playing outside, we had little interest in moving through space in a linear fashion from A to B. Time was fluid. You could encounter playful distractions in the landscape – a concrete hippo or mushroom to climb on. You might find sticks to pick up; objects to poke with a stick. You might sit down to observe a line of ants crawling across the pavement.

I remember following the sound of distant, ice-cream van chimes that would lead us through new routes in familiar streets. The van would eventually be found, nestling in one of the cul-de-sacs designed into the urban fabric, so that heavy traffic was largely separated from footpaths and safe for children.

I remember our weekly, Friday morning ritual. Dad would leave a cheque for 'the housekeeping' in the kitchen before he headed off to work. I would walk with Mum down to the town centre where we would stop at the bank to cash the cheque then go to the council office to pay our rent. I would pass over the book to get it stamped. We would then go for a treat in the Co-op cafe which was on a sort of mezzanine floor above the vast department store. My favourite treat was a finger roll with chopped egg, a cup of diluted orange juice and a strawberry tart afterwards.

I remember the strange looking statue that emerged from the ground in front of what became the bus station. As a child, I had the perception of this being a towering structure, but over the years it appeared to shrink. *Ex Terra* is a work by Benno Schotz and the first major work of public art in Glenrothes. It depicts a maternal figure emerging tree-like from the ground, symbolising the growth of the town from the earth itself.

I remember running around outside our house carrying a milk bottle. I fell and the bottle shattered with a lot of glass ending up in my hand. The doctor pulled it out with tweezers. I remember a shard coming out four years later when I was eight years old. It had travelled an inch inside my hand and part of it was now resting against a tendon in my wrist.

"It's been in there for half your life," the doctor said.

That evening, I watched a TV programme which had a rogue tiger pacing through rice fields, attacking and terrifying the local village.

I remember running away from home. I gathered up some belongings in a plastic carrier bag and matter-of-factly, told my parents I was running away. I went out the back door, no doubt being followed. I walked around the block and came in the front door.

I remember our second house in Caskieberran precinct. All these streets had some connection to Sir Walter Scott: Marmion Drive, Waverley Drive, Kenilworth Court, Abbotsford Drive. What effect did these signifiers have on the populace?

I remember the Caskieberran water tank, A grey monolith constructed at the highest point in the precinct. It towered over the landscape, a mystery in concrete with no obvious sign of entry or exit. What was it really for? – a question we all asked in the school playground. Perhaps, like an iceberg, it was the visible component of a vast, underground structure that constructed the hippos, mushrooms, heads and concrete henges that dotted our landscape. Or was it full of some mind-altering drug pumped through the water supply to create a compliant polis, bearing in mind that most folk had been transplanted from elsewhere in Scotland and thrown together on this greenfield site of former farmlands.

I remember that parts of the town were a huge construction site. New precincts were in the process of being built and colossal earthwork cuttings were gouged through the landscape which offered untold possibilities for play and mischief. A bridge, constructed of a scaffolded structure created a steel labyrinth climbing frame which we used to take great delight in crossing underneath, hanging by our arms from the highest point. We used to throw rocks from the bridge into the pooling water below and enjoy being chased off by the site workers.

I remember creating makeshift play dens in cornfields, where you could flatten down a rough circle and lie down without being seen.

I remember worrying about the mice as the bulldozers moved in on this field.

I remember going to the newly opened swimming pool,

when none of us could swim. We would walk down with trunks rolled up inside a towel carried underarm. You were given an orange box to put your clothes in and given a coloured armband. We usually had enough money left for a buttered roll in the canteen afterwards.

I remember the concrete hippos and mushrooms which dwelt amongst our precinct. Their presence made some people smile. They were created by the town's public artist which sounded like a good job to have. Over the years, as we travelled further into new precincts, we discovered concrete henges and temples, a cubist eagle, mural painted underpasses, a dinosaur, poetry paths, giant flowers and many other hidden curios.

I remember that each precinct had its own shop and TMR – the Tenants Meeting Room, a windowless concrete bunker which could be rented by the hour and hosted an array of community events such as Residents Association meetings, cubs, brownies, jumble sales and hobbyist groups. In adolescent years, these places were a godsend. Bands were formed and rehearsed on the weekends. Teenage discos were put on and first loves explored. In later teenage years, Davy Henderson's happening new band, from Edinburgh, The Fire Engines, came over to play in the Tanshall TMR.

I remember being sent to the precinct shop with a paper bag containing mum's collected cigarette coupons which could be exchanged for cash. It was only years later I realised that Mum was too ashamed of being seen cashing in her cigarette coupons. On a similar note, my brother and I were sworn to never tell our gran that Mum went to bingo on a Thursday night.

I remember our dog was always desperate to carry something back from the shop in its mouth. Giving it a newspaper was a bad idea, but a tin of spaghetti hoops or soup would make it ecstatic. Occasionally, he would drop the tin, nudge it along the pavement for a bit then pick it up and trot on.

I remember I once punctured a tin of macaroni with the tin opener and put it at the back in the food cupboard. When mum opened the tin the contents inside were covered in black mould. She wrote a letter of complaint to the food company and they sent us a box full of tinned food.

I remember a door- to-door salesman came around selling *Encyclopaedia Britannica*. You received the first volume free and paid the rest up on a weekly basis. We somehow managed to keep the first volume but no more came after that. I loved looking through it. For many years my general knowledge concentrated on things beginning A-ak.

I remember reading that J.G. Ballard once sold *Encyclopaedia Britannica* door-to-door.

I remember going up to the 'big school' called Glenwood High. Compared to primary school there were so many people as the catchment area pulled in several precincts and the surrounding towns of Leslie and Kinglassie. We were allocated into classes that spelt out G L E N R O T H E S. I was in IG. Glenwood was a typical 1960s modernist assemblage of fenestrated cubes, stacked on cuboids, to the extent that the same design was used for similar schools in Kirkcaldy and Dunfermline.

I remember some nicknames from school: Jacko, Ned, Clemy, Peerie, Beefy, Took, Wee T and Big T, Peekie, Camy, Kerrdo, Cush.

I remember sitting in history class when my English teacher knocked and entered, wanting to see me. I thought I was in trouble, but it turned out he wanted to publish a couple of my poems in the school magazine and one of the art teachers would draw something to accompany it.

I remember my morning paper round. Up at 6.00am. Rain, hail, sleet, slush, snow and sunshine. Freedom, moving through the landscape before the town had woken up. Dark cloaked mornings in winter. Beautiful fingers of light in summer.

I remember I had to deliver one copy of *The Financial Times*.

It would sit like a slice of pink luncheon meat sandwiched within the grey tower of *Daily Records* and *Couriers*. It was for a Mr Mason, who, many years later, I discovered was an acolyte of Margaret Thatcher and became known as 'the father of the Poll Tax'.

I remember our one-day wildcat strike at the paper shop. It was planned for maximum impact on a Thursday when the local paper – *The Glenrothes Gazette* – came out. We ended up being interviewed by *The Gazette* reporter and made the front page the following week. Our pay was increased from £1.25 a week to £1.75 a week.

I remember that following the paper round pay rise, I could buy an album every second week. I remember buying my first records and tapes from Woolworths and Forbuoys newsagent in the town centre. The Kingdom Shopping Centre, as it was known, but rarely referred to as such, was one of the earliest indoor shopping malls in Scotland.

I remember the revelation of discovering Glenwood public library, whose grey, concrete, brutalist exterior belied the colourful, exotic and fantastical worlds that could be accessed within. All those books, including a reference room with a complete set of *Encyclopaedia Britannica*! A universe of possibilities contained within four walls. The library, in conjunction with the *NME*, fostered a love of books and music which developed in tandem. I think it was Paul Morley who suggested that if Siouxsie and the Banshees were a writer they would be Kafka. These connections led me to the shelves and invariably the books were there to be borrowed.

I remember struggling through some Gurdjieff as Kate Bush mentioned him in a lyric, and the music and books connection was further cemented when local heroes from Dunfermline, the Skids, quoted Sartre on their debut LP, *Scared to Dance*. I remember Hugh MacDiarmid's poem *The Little White Rose* carved into a paving slab outside the library.

I remember buying a lurid red Corgi edition of *Catch 22* in

Forbuoys. Many years later, Joseph Heller signed that actual book for me.

I remember buildings in the town that looked as if they had arrived from the future. The Rothes Arms Hotel which resembled Thunderbird 5 with the circular Apollo Lounge. St Ninians church in Tanshall looked like a space station with two silver hexagonal structures on the roof and St Paul's church had the appearance of being constructed from white Lego bricks, unlike any traditional church design I had ever seen.

I remember finding out that St Paul's was designed by the firm of Gillespie Kidd and Coia who were also responsible for St Peter's Seminary, in Cardross, generally considered to be one of Scotland's most important modernist buildings.

I remember the original Brutalist grey cubes of council buildings and how green detailing around window frames can soften the most austere façade. When Brutalist windows can dream of trees and sky, framing swirling wisps of translucent cloud. A reflected cinema show of cumulus, breath and breeze.

I remember the sculptured flock of steel swifts, frozen in flight against tactile, concrete carpets of building cladding.

I remember looking old enough to get into the Apollo Lounge, which was a great place for seeing live bands with music on four nights a week. Programming was eclectic with a seemingly random stew of of punk, new wave, prog and metal appearing over any one week.

I remember my stand-out night in The Apollo was when an unheard-of band from Dundee appeared. The guitarist scythed into the opening number called *The Affectionate Punch* and we were introduced to the unique vocal gymnastics of Billy Mackenzie, sadly much missed. The band were called The Associates and Michael Dempsey from The Cure, played bass that night.

I remember it was years later when I realised that we had all lived in the same kind of houses, built in a small number of different styles. As council owned properties, the differentiating features were the interiors and cultural capital on display. One friend's parents were teachers who read *The Guardian* and had piles of books and magazines in their house, whilst my parents read *The Daily Record* and *The Courier*. I rarely saw either of them reading any book.

I remember when Margaret Thatcher started the right-to-buy property revolution and almost overnight, people began painting their front doors, digging up their gardens and installing double glazing.

I remember the town expanding south and northwards, with the building of new precincts such as Pitcoudie, Cadham and Balfarg. Balfarg is a portal gateway to the distant human past as it is built around a 6000-year-old ceremonial complex encompassing a circular timber and later stone henge enclosed by a circular ditch 65m in diameter. There are few sights as uncanny as this modern housing estate sitting around the perimeter of the still clearly delineated site of the stone circle.

I remember I had a summer job on one of the building sites. My dad was a sparkie involved in installing the central heating systems that went into the new houses. It was interesting to observe building site hierarchy and protocols between the clerk of works, foreman, sparkies, chippies, plumbers, brickies and, like me, the lowest of the low, the jobbing labourer. It was also a surprise to learn the rich lexicon of swear words that my dad used profusely on-site, which he rarely did in the house.

I remember that my job was to cut up huge yellow rolls of fibreglass wool which was used for loft insulation. The glass fibres had a knack of attaching themselves to every part of your body and thinking of this provokes a Pavlovian response to start scratching and the need to immerse myself in water.

I remember the River Leven that meandered through the town, thinking of its flowing waters coursing through the Fife landscape from Loch Leven near Kinross all the way to joining the Firth of Forth at Leven. Of powering linen mills and the local paper mills. Of sustaining the tadpoles and sticklebacks in the pond where we used to peer into the depths searching for those tiny flickering tails. What memories does this water now hold?

I remember thinking of beginnings and endings and what endures in between.

I remember attending an art exhibition in in Summerhall, Edinburgh, last year, and entering a room where Richard Demarco, the artist, curator and general cultural agitator was regaling an audience with a story about his collaborations with Joseph Beuys. I was later pulled into a conversation about Richard's book, *The Road to Meikle Seggie*, a personal account of his journey of artistic self-discovery on a road that leads nowhere but encompasses everywhere. It's partly grounded in a specific landscape on the outskirts of Milnathort. I mentioned that my father had grown up there and Richard asked me if I had ever lived in the town. I said that I had some distant memories, but we had moved to Glenrothes when I was a toddler. "Ah Glenrothes" said Richard, "do you know they named a street after me there? I'm in amongst Peploe, Eardley, Blackadder and MacTaggart.

"I do indeed" I said. My brother lives in Demarco Drive".

The land will always remember the standing stones, the farms, the New Town, the people who passed through...

Murdo Eason

Last Exit to Telford

Taxis tack the edges of towns,
stitch them to this patchwork city,
their work a double helix,
a glowing tapeworm strung out
along spinal road and motorway.

The curve, the swell, the arc,
the tight dark drum of its beat.

Old furnace, heat still in the soil,
dogwalkers and doggers skimming
this basalt plug of warm sea,
black stegosaurus hulking at dusk.

Land's palimpsest rewrites.
Once again traffic begins to slow
alongside three takeaways in a row.

Nick Pearson

Crow Valley Particulars

Mandy says that 'alight' isn't even a word, and that even if it is it's the kind of word that doesn't belong in a town like this. She says that people will be confused by it, that people round here are confused by most things at the best of times, and that it'll be just another reason for people to take the piss out of us.

'*Alight here for Cwmbran shopping!*' she snorts, between mouthfuls of Cherry Coke and sharp drags upon a crumpled B&H, 'as if!'. Her thick chestnut hair is patterned with traces of last night's gel and the buckles on her pointed boots twinkle in the winter sunshine as she leans back and stretches her legs towards *House of Fraser* so that everyone can see the ladders in her black tights that she's intentionally created. She's attached her own-brand *Walkman* to a pair of tinny speakers so that the new Bunnymen album can transform itself into a communal listening experience. The batteries have just given up the ghost though, so Gaz has gone to steal some more from Woolco.

Roger still sells loosies to her from an under-the-counter tin of panatellas at 10p a go. It's this more than anything else that has defined a 10p coin to be the acknowledged playground exchange rate since as far back as any of them can remember. Mandy's only been smoking for a couple of months, a period of time in which she's also taken to adding elaborate Cleopatra flourishes to the corners of her eye make-up. So many bangles and bracelets now adorn her spindly wrists that her slender alabaster arms have begun to resemble an unattended Victorian hoopla stall.

She has another group of friends these days, a collection of older kids who congregate down 'the bush' at lunchtimes and free periods; a sullen community of nicotine fiends whose existence has recently been given tacit approval by one of the senior teachers. The fastening of a Christmas card addressed "to all the smokers" to the centre of the eponymous shrub ultimately sealing the deal. As befits their roles as low-level urban subversives the smokers get Mandy into Newport nightclubs and routinely steal cassette tapes and aerosol cans to order. A black-market cottage industry whose fringe benefits filter down to even the lowest level of the school's social order. An accepted means of wealth distribution that takes place in the pungent shadows of obscenity-strewn bus stops and prefabricated Terrapin huts.

'Did you hear about them dopes who won a competition to be on the first journey from here to Newport?', she scoffs. 'Won a competition in *The Argus*, they did – *Why I want to be on the first ever train-ride from Cwmbran to Newport* – or some other such rubbish. Complete in no more than 12 words. It's not like it's winning the pools is it? Funny too that it should be a journey from here to Newport rather than the other way round. I can't see too many people from Newport wanting to "alight here", can you? The only reason people come to Cwmbran is for the free parking and who really gives a shit about that if you've travelled here by train in the first place. It don' make no sense'.

Jo tells her that it wasn't the first ever rail journey between the two towns, that there used to be a longstanding rail link that closed about twenty-five years ago; one that her Mum used to travel on as a child, but that it was axed just as the new town began to get into its stride. Since then it's mainly been used as a means of transporting freight between the north-west of England and Cardiff. A comforting nocturnal rumble that lulls Jo to sleep on the nights that she spends in the chilly back room of her grandparents' council home. The sweet release of sleep routinely losing out to the prospect of imminent nuclear war and why her period is so alarmingly late. Recently she's taken to pulling big chunks of hair from her head, the pony-tail that she's started to style her hair in more a means of masking the emerging patches of bare scalp than kind of personal style statement.

Mandy zips up her leather biker jacket, an impulsive mail order purchase from an ad in the back pages of the *NME*, until the zip brushes against the tip of her nose. She takes a final drag from her cigarette as she catches the eye of 'Dai and Myfanwy', wall-mounted figurine representations of what it supposedly means to be Welsh. An ugly stereotypical blight upon the pure concrete expanse that once encased the town's only theatre, the cold hard canvas upon which dreams of leaving could be idly sketched. Dai, a weary looking rural shepherd in the heart of a post-war new town, stands for everything that Mandy hates about living in South Wales in the 1980s; the creeping erosion of industry giving way to lazy Sunday afternoon nostalgia and the tendency to wallow in a past that seems totally alien to her in every way possible.

'Do androids dream of electric sheep?' she inks into her notebook.

'What are you writing in there?' Claire asks.

'Whassit to you?'

The inanimate and subservient Myfanwy looks down at Mandy, as if scolding her for her combative manner and her thoughtless treatment of Claire, of whom Mandy is genuinely fond.

'Oh, piss off Myfanwy'

'So, d'you gerrem then?'

'Course' Gaz grins, rummaging around in the crotch of his button-fly jeans before fishing out a double-pack of AA batteries and tossing them into Mandy's lap.

'Vile'

'I gorrem from Dixons in the end, it's like they were giving them away. It's even easier now than when I worked there on a Saturday. At least they don't frisk me on the way out now'

Mandy prizes open the back of her speakers and snaps in the batteries as Gaz drapes an arm over Claire's shoulder and cracks open a can of Fanta one-handed.

'Magic it was, at Dixons. I was like a kid in a sweet shop in that stock room. I'll never have to buy a C90 again'

Music tumbles out of the speakers and slides down the high-sloped red brick platform upon which they're all perched, a communal meeting space adjacent to the concrete bandstand, forever known to the town's teenage community as *The Wall*.

'There's some people who still refuse to believe we've even got a train station', Gaz says.

'Hughesy and his mate went on the train to watch the County the other week and took a battering off their own fans as they left Newport station'

'Huh?'

'Mad, innit? A bunch of their lads were looking to mix it with the away fans, not realising that Hughesy and his mate were actually County fans. They asked them what station they'd travelled from, it's what they always do, to suss out who's home and who's away, y'know. Hughesy told 'em "Cwmbran", to which one of them said, "there's no station there!". They got absolutely battered, Hughesy's mate ended up with a dislocated shoulder and a load of broken teeth'.

'Alight here for an absolute kicking', Mandy mutters.

'Savages', Claire spits. 'It's mad in Newport, absolute carnage, there's all kinds of headcases there. Some right bloody mad-'eads'.

'At least there are things happening there though, not like here. What have we got, eh? A couple of boring pubs and a McDonald's, it's hardly Vegas, is it?'

'Maybe not, Mand, but at least we can get served in the ones here. Gimmee the reliability of The Green over those snooty ones in Newport with their ID checks and their stupid doormen'.

'Unless you're banned, of course'.

'Piss off, Mand', Gaz grins back at her. 'I'd rather be a picket than a scab'.

'All I know,' Mandy says, her fingers fishing around in her bag for another cigarette. 'Is that this train line at least gives us one more option, another escape route'.

'Don't be like that, 'Mand'.

'It's all right for you, Claire, with your big house up Llanfrechfa and your exam results, you won't be sticking around here, you'll be fine. It's the rest of us who'll be scrabbling round for jobs at County Hall, if we're lucky, and Gateway if we're not'.

Everyone avoids Gazza's gaze and the yellow collar of his supermarket uniform that pokes out of the top of a red Tacchini jacket.

Claire lives in a 'big house up Llanfrechfa' on account of her father's longstanding job with the Cwmbran Development Corporation. Those post-war planners' dreams imbue every inch and of the town's hard concrete centre, each spiral staircase and flickering underpass strip-light standing as uncertain testament to a once noble vision.

'So it's his fault, is it?' Mandy's own father had once commented when dropping Claire off in his Nissan Sunny, a cheerful jibe typical of his good-natured sarcasm and an unerring suspicion of what he still refers to as 'the bankers' class'. The households that get *The New Statesman* delivered along with the morning paper, that eat salad out of wooden bowls, and whose white-collar pen-pushing jobs are so notoriously undemanding that they even allow them time to jostle for positions on the school's PTA - 'the Mafia of the meritocracy'. That's one of his, a phrase that Mandy had once used in an English essay and that had subsequently been questioned in red pen by a disdainful teacher who distrusted anything that did not emanate from the core syllabus laid down by the brown-suited autocrats of the Welsh Joint Education Committee.

'Off to London again, are you?' he'll often ask Claire, alert to her suspiciously frequent weekends spent in the capital.

'At my uncle's', she'll smile. 'He's got a flat in Chiswick, the

Welsh side. He's a great cook'.

Mandy says she's only ever heard Chiswick mentioned on Radio 1's traffic bulletins, that she's not sure that it's even a proper part of London, and that there's something not right about a middle-aged man living alone with only cats and recipe books for company.

'I'd take it though, she says, 'over here, I mean'.

'Take what?' Claire asks.

'London. Chiswick, even'.

'You mean to live?'

'Of course. It's all part of the plan. Give it a couple of years and I'm out of here'.

A recent edition of *The South Bank Show* was devoted to The Smiths and Mandy can't seem to get it out of her mind. It wasn't the music that necessarily captivated her, nor the tiresome pontificating of the sainted Morrissey who she'd never really taken to. She fell wholeheartedly instead for the band's celebration of the mundane, the use of period films to underline the theme, the glamorisation of boredom and the attendant allure of chucking it all in for another life beyond the limitations of a formulaic small-town existence. An objective best embodied by the sight of the goddess, Julie Christie, in *Billy Liar*, boarding a night train to London while the hapless Billy Fisher, rooted to the platform, cradles cartons of milk from a vending machine.

'Chiswick by 1988'.

'Whassat, Mand?'

'Chiswick by 1988, Mars by 1990'.

Jo says that it's about time Mandy knuckled down and started studying properly for her mocks. That she's the brightest girl in her French class by a country mile, but that the teachers are worried by the degree to which her interest has waned over the last few months.

'She's a law unto herself these days, mum. She got into a fight with another girl on the bus to Fairwater School last week and then tried to drown her in their bloody pool'.

'Silly bloody mare. I don't know what's got into her. She was such a quiet little girl too. Wouldn't say boo to a goose when you were in juniors with her'.

Jo stands in front of the mirror and parts her hair down the centre with a steel comb, an exposed patch of rosy skin at the crown briefly catching the light as she lowers her head for its daily inspection.

'Her father works at Girlings too, doesn't he?' her mother asks from behind the kitchen door.

'Used to. He took redundancy at the end of last year. Too good to turn down apparently. He just spends his time kicking round the house now. That and driving round town in his beaten-up car. The blue one with the mustard door. You must have seen it?'

'That's *his* car?'

'Yeah', Jo laughs.

'We see him all the time when we walk into town. Constantly going around the roundabouts, always on his own, no idea where he's off to. Not sure if he even knows. We can't joke about it though, not in front of Mandy. She'd go spare'.

'Have you told them yet, love?'

'About the scholarship? Ha. No. They don't even know that I applied. Nothing's officially confirmed yet, mum. Let's not tempt fate, eh? I'd prefer just to keep it to myself for now'.

'Don't be so negative, love. This is the chance of a lifetime, it could open so many doors for you. I want you to have the future we were all promised when your Nan and Grampa first moved here. Somewhere bright and shiny and new. The bloody space age! I don't want you sat behind a typewriter in County Hall or stamping passports in Newport for a living. There's a big world out there, and people like us don't get offered these kinds of opportunities very often. Keep your head down if you like. You'll know soon enough'.

Jo bites her lip and drags the length of the steel comb down the patch of exposed skin until she feels the pressure give and the slow release of a small trickle of blood. Elton John's 'Your Song' plays quietly in the background, a black and yellow paper label rotating beneath the scratched smoked glass lid of a Ferguson turntable. For Jo, there's no song more evocative of childhood than this, a sun-dappled memory of falling asleep in the back of her father's Fiat as it negotiated the narrow lanes between St. Ives and Falmouth in faltering light. Her sleeping head rested against the bony shoulder of an older sister. A cartridge player filling the tiny space with the tinny sounds of one decade segueing into another. Parsley, sage, rosemary and thyme. A tiny Italian car full of rocket men and killer queens.

———————

Sally leaving home for college in '84 felt like the clanging death knell of childhood though. When she later decided to put permanent roots down in Sheffield the once impregnable sisterly bond that they had always shared began to slowly atrophy. Each passing day a scornful rejoinder to the faded photograph of them both in the gold frame that sits above the fireplace in defiance of reality; two sisters captured forever in a jumble of seaside arms, ice cream cones and crooked teeth. Jo dabs at the wound with a fingertip, smearing its rosy residue across the back of a hand before sweeping her hair across.

'I'll go and pack, shall I?'

'You've got the entire week to do that, love'.

'I think I'll do it now though. I think I'll go and pack'.

On the same morning that the Health Minister, Edwina Currie, announces that 'good Christians don't die of AIDS'. Jo listens intently from behind the bathroom door as her mother seeks to convince a disbelieving Mandy that she's gone out and that she doesn't know when she'll be back. As soon as the coast is clear Jo steps aboard a yellow Bustler at the bottom of Llanyrafon Way, handing over a 20p coin and secluding herself amongst the gaggle of pensioners, young mothers, and their feral kids. She buries her chin into the zipped collar of her jacket and clamps a pair of lightweight headphones to her ears as the funny-looking yellow bus ambles its way past the hulking factories of *Saunders Valves* and *Lucas Girling* before finally coming to a halt in the town's bus station. She lifts off her bag, slings it across a shoulder and makes her way towards Glyndwr Road, the cold February wind eating into her dry red cheeks. Picking up the pace, the railway station only a short walk away now, the music that envelops her seems to be sporadically interspersed with the voices of her friends and her family; her mother, her sister, Claire, Gaz, and of course Mandy; all of them calling out her name with increasing degrees of desperation.

'Jo!'

'Jo. Love!'

'Jo-Jo!'

Jo! Jo! You silly cow!'

Mandy?

Jo's running now, harder and faster, propelling herself forward, determined not to look behind or to fret about the icy wind that cuts through her fine hair and into the exposed patches of her scalp.

'Jo! Slow down! Jo!'

The railway station is gradually coming into view now, the pointed roof of its red-brick ticket office and its ugly metallic bridge. Jo snatches a glance at the face of her digital watch. Only minutes to go, but just enough time to purchase a ticket, gather her thoughts, and lose herself within the small northbound huddle doing whatever the opposite of 'alighting' is. Jo drops down into the car-park, gasping for air, before relenting and looking back for one final time.

Mandy? Could it be? Really?

'Jo!' she half-heartedly shouts, her voice cracked, her shoulders slumped, her fingers tightly grasping whatever it is that she's carrying. A plastic lighter, a packet of cigarettes, and a carton of milk.

Craig Austin

Bracknell

Overspilling from London
into leaf feathered lanes
and gated estates.
Nocturne's hallowed blanket
is pierced by the circling
and droning of jumbos,
these spray painting vandals
chemtrailing the clouds.

Eight thirty at night
and these monuments to crudeness
lie hollow and lightless,
the keys to the castle
still toiling in Toytown,
to pay for a lifestyle
there aren't enough hours for.

Wake, travel, work, sleep.
Wake, travel, work, sleep.

Harry Gallagher

An Embarrassment of Roundabouts – Redditch New Town

Needles and fish hooks. This is what Redditch was best known for before it became a new town in the second half of the last century. Needles, fishing tackle and light engineering – springs, engine parts, motorcycles (Royal Enfield, their motto: 'Made like a gun'), nickel-cadmium batteries, aircraft components. But it was needle production that made the town an industry that drew many to labour in its workshops in the late medieval period. It has been estimated that Redditch gave the world up to 90% of its needles in its manufacturing prime. It was a powerful image to think of so many simultaneously squinting into the tiny abysses of innumerable shards of steel that all began life in the same unassuming Midlands town. A town of sharp things; even the water power that drove the needle-scouring machinery came from a river called the Arrow, not that it was especially straight or true.

The town went unmentioned in the Domesday Book: Redditch did not exist as an entity back in 1086, although the villages and hamlets that would later fall under the authority of its borough council were noted – Anglo-Saxon 'leys' like Beoley, Studley, Bentley and Batchley. And Bordesley, which held Bordesley Abbey, a Cistercian institution founded in the 12th century that prospered for centuries before being disestablished in the reign of Henry VIII.

The area was already well connected in pre-Conquest times. A Roman road, Icknield Street, passed a little way east of what would later become the town centre, and there were long-established salt ways that ran from Droitwich to the west. By the 13th century, a market centre had developed where the routes between Birmingham and Evesham, and Kidderminster and Warwick intersected. The settlement at the crossroads here would eventually grow to become the market town of Redditch.

A medium-sized market town in the Midlands, a place of small factories and modest ambitions, with Victorian civic buildings at its core, Redditch – 'Red-ditch' – took its name from the glutinous red clay that underlay the region and hampered drainage in suburban gardens. Some liked to imagine that the name derived from a fraught English Civil War battle in which the ditches flowed red with blood but this was mere fancy – it was a matter of iron-rich glacial deposits rather than steel-cut gore. Even so, if you looked hard enough there were hints of an older, eldritch England lurking beneath the surface, and the town's rural hinterland was replete with tales of ghostly presences, haunted lanes and 'grey lady' apparitions. With districts of the old town going under spooky names like Headless Cross, it was inevitable that spectral back stories would have to be invented even if they did not exist already.

Although I was born on the edge of the Black Country, I spent the first few years of my life in the countryside southwest of Birmingham. Then when I was five we moved to Redditch, first to the aforementioned Headless Cross, whose name did not strike me as particularly macabre at the time (although it did later inspire a Black Sabbath song of the same name), and then in my teens to a green belt suburb at the town's western fringe. Here we lived along a leafy lane which, after the last house had been passed, plunged abruptly into bucolic countryside. It was a location that boasted long views across fields to the distant whaleback of the Malvern Hills, a place where, if you listened closely enough, the strains of both Elgar and Led Zeppelin[2] might just be discerned on the breeze – priapic heavy metal melding with pastoral nostalgia.

---

[2]Led Zeppelin's John Bonham, considered to be one of the greatest rock drummers of all time, was a native of Redditch and probably the town's most famous son. A statue depicting Bonham in full flow at his drum kit was erected in 2018 on the church green in the town centre.

Redditch in those days still retained the air of a small market town. Birmingham, just 15 miles up the road, seemed distant – a place for special occasions, shopping trips, rock concerts, culture grabs. With rolling pasture land of sheep and cows nudging its periphery, and golf links and woodland separating the housing zones closer to the centre, Redditch back then still had a vague whiff of the farmyard about it – prime territory for The Archers back-story just down the road in make-believe Borsetshire.

The town was earmarked for expansion as part of the second wave of the 1946 New Towns Act, and in 1964 the newly created Redditch Development Corporation set about fulfilling its vision. There were already a few housing estates in place around the Victorian town centre. Some of these, like Abbeydale, Mayfields and Batchley, were post-war council stock, while others were privately owned cul-de-sacs of 1950s aspiration, their roads given the names of poets to conjure the right sort of cultural associations: Coleridge Close, Tennyson Road, Byron Road, Swinburne Road, Wordsworth Avenue. Only 19th-century Romantics would suffice – we were, after all, close enough to the Bard's birthplace at Stratford-upon-Avon for our English teacher to assume that, as a matter of geographical determinism, we would be able to imbibe fine language by osmosis. She was invariably disappointed.

How she despaired at our mangled vowels and bludgeoned grammar, our small town insularity, our indifference to what we perceived as a milieu too hifalutin for the likes of us. The Shakespeare that most of her doggedly unenthusiastic pupils were more likely to know was Norris-Shakespeare, then the town's principal fishing tackle factory.

The most dramatic transformation that took place in the genesis of the new town could probably be dated to the opening of the new dual-carriageway. This state-of-the-art traffic system was designed to channel motorists around the town centre, although the trouble was it also had a tendency to whisk them speedily out of town before they even knew it. As the then popular Birmingham comedian Jasper Carott gently mocked in his stand-up routine, it was easier to visit Bromsgrove from Redditch than Redditch itself. The new road system was bold and large-scale, almost Soviet in its ambition. It seemed a zone where it was possible to drive for miles, obediently following signs and spinning around roundabouts, to arrive back at the same starting point with absolutely no knowledge of where you had just been. Urban myths that told of hapless motorists locked in ring-road limbo for hours seemed quite believable.

As well as a plethora of roundabouts to siphon-off estate dwellers from their work commute, the system incorporated what was then England's only cloverleaf interchange – an array of curling asphalt that must have looked impressive from the air, a useful route marker for migrating geese. Such was the extent of the new road system that a joke went round that the Redditch Development Corporation was determined to offer a dual carriageway for each and every resident. Certainly there was capacity, more than sufficient for any future development and expansion. There still is.

The new roundabouts quickly became part of the local mythos – confusing, uncountable way-stations along a Möbius strip of road that, for the inexperienced, seemed to inevitably lead back to the same starting place. The seemingly endless parade of roundabouts (actually, about 40) soon became the go-to joke for out-of-town Midlanders, as well as a source of grudging affection for locals. A Redditch company, BB Print Digital, even went as far as producing a calendar of them in 2002, when company director Kevin Beresford stated that he viewed Redditch's multiple roundabouts as 'an oasis in a sea of asphalt', although no one was able to identify exactly how tongue-in-cheek he had been when he said this. The calendar, which soon became a cult classic, sold up to 2,000 copies a year at the height of its popularity. Beresford, who founded the Roundabout Appreciation Society around the same time as this marketing venture, would go on to make an appearance himself in the 2015 *Dull Men of Great Britain* calendar.

In tandem with the expansion of the traffic circulatory system, the town centre (if you could find it) was given a complicated one-way system that made use of pre-existing roads. This newly enforced direction of travel disorientated locals used to more direct transits across town.

I have a vague memory of one case outlined in the *Redditch Advertiser* in which a local pub landlord, whose property lay at the corner of two roads, was obliged to drive for over a mile to travel between his front and back doors. This may be merely poorly remembered apocrypha on my part but it has the ring of plausibility about it. What was undeniable was that almost overnight the territory had changed significantly; mental maps needed to be redrawn; long-held homing instincts could no longer be relied upon.

Another leap forward for the ever-expanding new town came with the opening of the Kingfisher Shopping Centre in 1976, whose echoing retail acreage took over a chunk of the old town centre. The centre achieved instant recognition for its novel incorporation of living palm trees imported from Spain into the central exhibition space of Worcester Square.

At a time when Mediterranean package holidays were becoming the norm for working class families, there was a resonance here with palms and concrete, a shopping experience (gleefully promoted with the tagline 'Shopping under the palms') that echoed happy times of sangria, paella and high-rise concrete on the Costa del Sol. For those with sufficient imagination it was a non-space transformed to pleasure dome, an exotic deposit of cultural capital in the beating heart of the commercial zone.

The original palm trees – just six to start with – had arrived like grumpy rock stars on separate flat-bed lorries and had to be coaxed painstakingly into their interior space.

Townsfolk came out to watch their arrival – it was the greatest live event in Redditch since Princess Margaret had done a hand-waving drive-by through the town in the early 60s. The palms, which sprouted from massive pots, did not exactly thrive but managed to stay alive for the next three decades, eventually outgrowing the limited space at their disposal.

They were finally removed for reasons of health and safety in 2005. Their replacements were of a different species – the original date palms substituted with more suitable Washingtonia Robusta – although no one really seemed to notice.

By the time the Redditch Development Corporation had reached its sell-by date in 1985 the town population had increased to 74,000, more than doubling over the 21 years of the corporation's existence. The Redditch of old was no longer; the town's gravity had shifted. There were cultural shifts to consider too: a population increasingly dominated by incomers from Birmingham and the New Commonwealth, and a dilution of the singular local accent – Brummie argot had become the new lingua franca.

The idea back in 1964 – a commendable enough vision – had been that each new housing area would be developed as a separate village, each with a mix of private and rented accommodation and its own infrastructure, shopping area, pubs, services and schools. What was unforeseen was the increasing role that the private car would play in family life, with estate dwellers eager to drive from their own locality to out-of-town supermarkets and the like for shopping and leisure.

As a result some local shops did not survive, while estate pubs went out of business and ended up being boarded-up and abandoned. Quick to seize an opportunity when it presented itself, Kevin Beresford of roundabout calendar fame would go on to publish a *Perished Pubs of Redditch* calendar in 2017.

I left Redditch after 'A' levels to go to what was then a polytechnic in Coventry, an hour's drive away. Within 15 months, unhappy with my degree course and the urban malaise the city engendered in me, I was back, temporarily, at least. This, I suppose, was my gap year, although such a thing did not really exist in those days.

I returned to live with my parents and worked for a few months as a postman, getting up at an unearthly hour to sort mail in the town centre sorting office before being dropped off on my round in one of the less salubrious parts of the new town. Post office protocol dictated that the younger the staff member, the further they could walk, and so as a junior employee I was obliged to traipse for hours on long rounds around the flats and maisonettes of a north Redditch council estate.

It was a homecoming of sorts but one that engendered a mild sense of queasiness. I could never quite return to the life that I had before. It felt like a retrograde move: I had moved on while my small, old town world – parents, school friends, the pubs I frequented – had remained seemingly frozen in time. But beyond this, it was not the same place at all. In my absence the new town's relentless expansion had continued apace and I found myself experiencing a degree of disorientation each time I left the comfort zone of the town centre.

As it was, my postman's round was in a part of town that I had never really got to grips with – an unfamiliar housing zone that lay at the end of a ring-road byway. Having spun me centripetally out of the town in the first place, Redditch's bewildering road system now led me into a foreign land closer to home. Untested, unmapped, this was 'Here be Dragons' territory for a green-belt college boy like me.

The estate to which I delivered was only a few years old but already starting to crumble – the housing substandard, its residents poor and often unemployed, a portent of the Thatcher years to come. My clearest memory is of packs of feral dogs roaming the streets around the flats, aggressive protectors of their circumstantial territory. A baptism of fire of sorts, the experience toughened me up and the daily regime of an eight-mile urban trudge burdened with two bulging, cross-strapped mail bags served me well as training for later backpacking ventures abroad.

I worked on the post long enough to save up a little money before hitchhiking to Greece in the late spring. My first full-time job, my first solo travel, the post office was my launch pad as a would-be explorer and man of letters. Redditch New Town was my training ground as world traveller, the first terra incognita I would learn to deal with.

After this, I moved away from the town for good but returned periodically to visit friends and family. Each time I went back, Redditch seemed a little more changed, a little more unfamiliar and less like home. Almost invariably, on driving in from the north, I would become lost. With memory faded and instincts modified by dealings with more intuitive, albeit congested, road layouts, the Redditch road system's powers of confusion never seemed to diminish. The ring road, inevitably, was the wrong road. A sat nav may have been of use, but my geographical instincts, honed in more innocent times, were no longer of any value.

An oft-practised psychogeography technique, one guaranteed to disorientate and bring fresh insight to the urban dérive, is to navigate by means of using a map of a different town or city. Something similar might also be achieved by utilising a map from another time – the mental map I still carried within me from the Redditch of my formative years, a map which had never been upgraded to include the new thoroughfares, one-way systems and vast housing estates that orbited the centre; a map coloured by nostalgia and faded memory that had long since outgrown its utility.

Laurence Mitchell

Galleries, Washington

So I've told my daughter's mum I'll try
to sort the school shoes this time, conscious
I'm in the red on this one and knowing
there's always some other bits and pieces
plus the absolute ball-ache of considering
whether to walk through all that, walk through
all those cars and vans and car parks and roads
or drive the Vauxhall tank and stop at stop lines
and reverse, go backwards again and again as
much reversing is required to face the right way
always bloody back-tracking I seem to be
and I need to phone and check some details
about the shoes and the chance of returns
and whether there's another one of these
in the city or whether I'll need to come back
for the return I know there'll be an effing return

Rob Walton

Apollo Landing

I felt the future you dreamt of, then,
and many other times, too,
travelling north to roll eggs down Penshaw Hill
and drink Double Maxim in The Ivy,
silver wallet of freshly opened Silk Cut.
Everything square and new as we drove
through the jet cutting sliced in the rock.

At Peterlee, the perfect place
for catalogue sales and dark bouffant hair,
Marilyn pulls up in a red automatic,
lets the morning air pimple tanned legs.
Under the rough wash sky, moor-grey and slatey,
two-thirds deep, windowed boxes face
the snake charm green, turn towards the light,
unblindfolded. North wind force unbroken
across cheap felt.

Are we still in the place we said we would be?
Or, like these roads set along contours, crossing
seams and fault lines, on separate journeys?
I hear the echoes of men fragment
down smutty tunnels, snag at lift-shafts.

Breaking from the side of the Pavilion,
a bird begs for food, open jaw clamps.
The steps to the temple thin, worn by Roman
sandals. We sit on the stone bench
as on a rooftop baked in Mediterranean heat
or the primitive bed in a prison. We watch
the man lean to kiss his wife, their heads
two flat black circles. How their bodies curl,
shadowing the corners of the wall.

The lollipop totem rises from the pool

and when the rain is heavy enough, pushes
through serrated teeth, grooved silver,
overflows the portcullis.

The grey heart fades into the column
leaves me unpestered by things I will not let in.

Helen Angell

While Visiting

None of the side roads are wide enough
to turn around in. No change allowed
in this purpose-built, now car-dense town.
Finally, I find a space, stop, park, get out.

At my feet, part of Welwyn Garden City
floats in muddy-puddled fragments.
Winter leaves drift like rudderless boats.

I stand inside a giant bauble of Christmas lights
outside the shopping centre, and look up
at the sky – wide, quiet and still
through the wire net of sparkling.

The moon is whole and bright tonight.
It knows this place like no one else can,
the labyrinth of streets and lives.

My darker side has its own maze,
purpose hidden at the centre,
not even the moon knows
where to find it.

Next morning, I draw the hotel curtains
and gaze out at a small park,
where a woman is walking her dog.
There's purpose in her dawn stride,
like she's unwrapping her day –
its gift hers alone, the paper
laid out as green space.

I walk my thoughts with her,
and realise the marbled blue sky
is a window, curtains left open –

the purpose-built town below

busy simply in the purpose of being,
living life as it comes.
I watch, breathe, smile.

Sarah James

Overspill

Rainy Saturday afternoons

winds ripple coffee over puddles. Below privet,
slugs stream out among an elaborate calligraphy
of dogshit and cigarette ends, the discarded and
    unwelcome.

Behind lines and thresholds, reproduction masters
hang in gilded frames. Chintz,
Wedgewood kept for best,
plastic imitating willow, to hold prizes of Golden
    Delicious.

In the kitchens, Five Spice, Angel Delight,
a brick of Neapolitan wrapped in newspaper,
crouches low in the cool beneath Formica.

Radios speak into silence.

At night, the old country seeps back into the estate,
a new-born place, abstract finding form. Foxes root
beneath manicured hedges and turn over ashcans.
Moths ghost around sodium lights,
mist hovers over lawns.
Spirits laugh in dark alleys, and whistle down
    chimneys.

When they first arrive, children walk the streets,
spying on houses of ones they think better off,
those only joined to one other,
or even completely detached;
eying interiors, rooms with spaces in the middle of
    them.
In winter, it is at its harshest, the most unforgiving.
Stone statues squatting by gateposts,
bulbs pricking the soil like neatly stitched seams,
blackened branches of plum and cherry reaching

for a watercolour sun. The edges punctuated
by a shock of red; a phone box or an idling postvan.

At the boundary, more open to the sky,
a spit of wildwood, elder, and spindle,
treading mythical lines, along the periphery.

To stand here is like peering over the rim of the world
into a fairy-tale. Only the post-box, for some reason placed
at the end, on the wrong side of the road, stands like
a crimson exclamation mark, in solidarity with suburban sprawl

New-borns need to find their own patterns and rituals,
the lineation of milk bottles on steps, washing flying
early as possible to beat the neighbours in a competition
that was always unspoken. Its heartbeat becomes rhythms
of daily chores, conversations over chestnut palings, chain-link,
the ongoing geometry of connection and distance.

New people cannot be avoided, made insubstantial
by bricks and mortar. They cluster and constellate;
meteorites travelling far from their origins. Imagine them,
stepping home from work into waiting warm slippers,
unwinding in cool gardens that smell of lavender and honeysuckle.

At twilight, stars appearing, maybe someone raises a hand,

as if to touch their brightness, the sky here so much clearer
than damp squibs spied through London smog.

What is a home anyway? A place with four walls, and a roof,
with your people and things in it, a place to lay your head.

A place that doesn't threaten to collapse and wall you up in dust.
Separation is deception, there is simplicity in taking people,

lifting them out and placing them elsewhere.
Distance is a long thread
that pulls in a new town, all factories, farming, warehouses, shift patterns,

shopkeepers, safety boots. Happiness is implied.
Here is your own house.
You will have a garden, clear air, jobs,
here is a fresh start.

Maybe moving was like picking at the edges of an old wound,
or ripping a plaster off too quickly and taking the scab away with it.

At night, in empty roads,
a chorus of wings passes over dark rooftops,
fields beyond stretch silently, and at a window a single bulb burns

where someone sits up late, sips tea; remembers.

Alison Jones

Harlow 1971

Pantomime at the pristine
Playhouse.
Exciting new dramas.
Houses with white doors,
and clean bricks.
Families relocated from
Waltham Cross.
A home with three floors?!
So
many stairs!

A townhouse?!
We're not *in*
        a town;
Not a *real*
        one!

Children play outside,
get O levels at a brand
new school.

Flat roofed pubs,
named after butterflies,
crop up everywhere.
Finally, somewhere to go
on Sunday night.

Buying school uniform from
The High Shopping Centre;
They have a C&A!

Fresh slate,
gleaming paintwork
and radiant signs
for roads that seem to

go on forever.
We get lost.
Too many roundabouts.
They say there's an Old Harlow.
But I'm sure that's impossible.

Heather Moulson

From a Ford Zephyr six

well it happened like this;
an Act of Parliament, caused
the Birmingham diaspora to breathe out
and the second wave crackled like a spreading fire
away from bomb sites and blackened bricks
for a space to flourish
in open country
that's how it was.

Dora is all for space and flourish
past gardens and shopping parades and then round again,
she pats her Ford Zephyr when she parks, with the engine ticking,
hem lines, chrome door handles, the west wind, the vortex of the new age,
with the pound in her pocket
she drives all day Monday
for the luxury,
she drops a gear

tests the fabric of the landscape
the pull in the pit of her stomach is the future
where Redditch becomes the midwest, freeways and fly overs
she opens her up along the dual carriageway
and gasps at weightlessness,
and has giddying glimpses of the spinning, tumbling fields,
nearing the speed of sound. Under a cloud spun sky,
the swoon of the cloverleaf,

the giddy symmetric whorl of the curve
tensioned by an occipital wrench

like the Nazca lines or an iron age barrow
only understood from above.
The laws of physics still apply by the road side
the archaeological sedimentary ring, bottles and cans. Further out
the baling twine and pieces of plastic without function or form
and her discarded cigarette lighter, still slightly warm,

into fourth and she glances up at the couple on the bridge
who see the silver blur of a Zephyr's fins
and both raise a hand
so quickly the approach becomes the past
in a roar of engine noise, they think she was waving
she thinks they were waving, but it is over so fast,
a chiffon scarf maybe, they say, a little fast for the cloverleaf they say,
surging to the event horizon.

Brian Comber

Rabbit Run

They tried to paste a Telford sticker
on the existing places,
stick houses and steel warehouses
on the industrial remnants and dry canals.
They planned a spiral of treelined roads,
formulated a warren of footpaths linked in tunnels
designed by horror film location units.

> The trees have outgrown the plastic rabbit
> guards
linking to local woods and you're now
more likely to see a deer than a traffic light
which sparks an argument on the panther
I saw on the A4169 one late night return, eyes alert
> for blue lights.

> And in the middle of this modernity
Blist Hill Victorian Town,
smelling of Bakers and Candle Makers,
hissing and clinking on every corner,
where I puzzled on the bloke on his haunches
between the empty pigeon lofts
doing now't under his flat cap
waiting to be in a poem as I puzzled
if he was being paid to look unemployed

And on Saturdays the town park
wiggles with 5K joggers
who cat walk back through the Shopping Centre
past the grey pyjama tracky bottoms
of the munching rabbits
free from local hutches.

Steve Harrison

Map of Llandarcy / Coed Darcy 2008

And they stripped her layer by layer:
routes; networks; arteries
that stretched beyond her place.

Men's blistered fingers,
sweat-filled eyes, raw soles
removed from sight.

Still the scars, from a distance.
The echoes of lives that burnt
calligraphic forms.

Their blood runs deep,
the now routine turning of sod,
fathomless.

History flows to Crymlyn Bog,
silenced beneath the pristine concrete cap,
still thick, with elemental toil.

Marcelle Newbold

Screwfix

What are those trees under the concrete bridge; those evergreen leaves that droop over the path and brush my face by the riverside; those grand fortresses of corrugated steel; those white lampposts shaped with seaside ornateness; those stainless palisades that keep no-one in and no-one out of secret carparks?

I see them every day, but I have no answers. I know so little of this place that I've called home for all my twenty-nine years, and it knows even less of me.

I first became disassociated when I was fourteen. Reality forsook its concreteness, and instead began to swim with something malignant. The shape of things turned wrong. The outline of a plastic bottle came to represent a threat, and a reminder that someone somewhere made decisions I couldn't understand; decisions that seemed to determine the way things looked and were, no matter that they could be any other way if those in-charge really wanted them to be.

It was these alternatives- these other ways- that loomed; that held burning sway over me and seemed to be shooting through everything that met my gaze even momentarily. I spent most days with my eyes screwed shut, trying to forget everything but the person I was before the change. It was no use. In all of my last childhood afternoons, the sun now shone as it never should; the chalk outlines on the pavement shifted in dimensions, growing larger and smaller with each glance; my house tilted and swayed in the winds of an entirely still day, and shadows touched the ground at impossible angles.

I can remember the doctor my mother made me go and see when I refused to get out of bed or switch on the lights. I remember his desk painted a blinding white, his white blazer and his white jeans. What was he wearing, and why? He looked at me hard across the desk with amber eyes and big bushy eyebrows.

"It's just chemicals, you know. Things out of whack."

He slid the prescription paper towards me across the slickly painted wood.

"This will help. They'll bring you back to us a little. Other than that, plenty of exercise. Go for walks. Soak it all in. You're too young to get hung up on the nature of things; try and accept it all for what it is."

He was the same as the rest of them, as all the brainiacs to come. Soft and complacent and content. They could never accept that a place could do this to people; that a place could strand people outside of itself and themselves while still tying them tightly to the contours of the land.

Everyone who comes to Welwyn Garden City says there's something off about it. My ex-boyfriends always seemed ill-at-ease here, and walked between the semi-functional train station and the town centre, down the riverbank and through the rainbow-daubed underpasses, in states of near-mute drowsiness. One lad- of a more poetic bent- seemed the most troubled, and I remember him standing once on a bridge over a main road, looking back at the silent silhouette of a newbuild office with a sloped roof and shadowed windows.

"No-one's ever been in there," he'd said, the thought and his voice sailing in from somewhere far off.

"Why do you say that?"

"Look at it. It's too quiet. People can't- don't- pass through a place and leave no trace. There'd be a sign somewhere- something out of place, or moved, or broken. A door that doesn't close properly, or a van blocking an exit. No. There's nothing. It's not right."

He was trembling.

It's true that once-and-future suburbanites always speak lowly of their hometowns. They struggle in mumbling tones for the right words to express the inexplicable drabness. But what they never realise is that their unutterables aren't even worth the effort to begin with. They don't know the half of it, not really. They don't know what it's like to live here. They haven't had to reflect on the last remnants of forgotten civic pride; the torn-up lawns and greying fountains of the exact same age and history and meaning. They haven't had to know these relics will be bulldozed soon as well, to allow buildings of even obscurer purpose to roost on the rubble. Their worlds are dull but safe. Change is marked in hard outlines and remembered clearly. Every dowdy thing has a reason for its being and is used at it should be. It's not like here, not at all.

I walk most days. I have little else to do. I walk through the zones that separate and mix themselves; down the long rows of detached houses, home to moderately successful city managers; alongside the Shredded Wheat factory, that demon of towering pipes and sharp edges that crouches just beyond John Lewis; between the comfortless warrens of overbuilt streets called Goblins Green and Athelstan Walk, and over the low hills that hide the memory of thin brick chimneys endlessly pumping smoke, and keep from current view the rain-beaten horror of a Screwfix store large and dark.

I walk through these things that seem unreal as a daily test, or as a sort of fortification. I've had periods of restfulness, of normalcy, but even then, I was just waiting to fall again. A single blink at the wrong moment could make everything incorrect. If I was to sit on a bench by one of the brown-brick churches, I could perhaps see the old sinister dreams once more, beckoning through the rain or loop-the-looping round the unholy municipal spire.

I used to look at the black and shit-stained bust of Louis de Soissons, our beloved town architect; the memorial to Ebenezer Howard; and the crowds leaving the blank expanse of Sainsbury's, and feel my old thoughts about bottles and chairs and pavements deepen.

What I came to realize was that I've never really wanted or

longed for anything- not even a release from this thing in me. I think I've been stripped of those urges.

All this time my life has not been my own. I have lived only in the needs and desires of others. The men remembered in engraved stone and plaster built this place to prove themselves and their great ideas. They directed the lives of the families who came to populate this theory-in-action, this fantasy in tarmac and grass, only towards the proving or disproving of the worth of a life's work. I am disproof. Others, content in their spacious living rooms and paid-off BMW's and Sunday John Lewis hikes, are the opposite: they validate and confirm.

Eventually, the old men will know for certain whether they were right and good or not: one type will win over the other, and the town will either sing with communal and council-approved rapture or see all its people flee. The dirty busts will stay up, cleaned and gleaming, or come down for good.

There's no path to recovery for me. I continue as a piecemeal subject of a larger experiment, and I go across the town from green to brown to grey and back again. There's little left to discover, and there might not have been much to begin with, not beyond what it took me fifteen years or so of collapse to find. I don't really touch, and I remain untouched.

Except that soon, the Shredded Wheat factory will be brought down entirely, and I fear whatever shadows are still left on this ground will go with it. Afterward, I suppose we'll just be left with an eternal Screwfix of the soul. But perhaps, in days yet to come, the steel skeletons of those warehouses and retail complexes will be all that remains of the town. And maybe long-distant Welwynites will look upon those hulking edifices and think them the tombs and monuments of a race of Giants. God, I hope so. There must be a magic that's not just in my mind, or in the street names that lie in thick black lettering about Athelstan walking, and yearnings by the mount, and Goblin's cavorting until the fiery footsteps of the

Saxon King chase them back into the safety of their two-car garages and allotment sheds.

WELWYN GARDEN CITY: CITY SHOPPING IN THE COUNTRY
WELWYN GARDEN CITY: WAITING FOR TWILIGHT

Billy Stanton

The Roundabouts of Telford

Noughts once pencilled on a page.

Cogs to turn and hold
a balance of the generations.

Capstans of renewal
spooling out their ropes of road
to bind old with new,
knot buried seam to rising gleam.

Flywheels for an apartheid of age
pulling last century ways
through dartboard pubs
and drags of red-brick rarity shops.

Spinning plates of plenty
loading retail parks and mall
for baristas to tame the steam
of young and hopeful money.

Clock face collage for Google Earth,
Catherine wheels of light
for those who fly in the dark.

Crop circles come to live in town.

Nick Pearson

Glimpse

I turned away from vain staring down the line
for a train that would not come
and found trees beyond the station
viewed from Bracknell's municipal greyness
their greens were varied and splendid
their depth intriguing
a beckoning call to some other place.
I probably saw wasteland
"Soon to be redeveloped"
but, for second or two, it was Faery.
Then the train came.

Kim Whysall-Hammond

Cumbernauld [3]

Ma Granny did say I'd like it. Said she was jealous an aw. Telt me there wis loads of room tae run about, not like oor auld street. And she's right. Oh it's great so it is, a pure palace. All sparkling like oor shoes on Sun kneeling in the church. Da makes us clean them, newspaper folded on the shiny lino. Sunday Post. Best is when you get the bit inside with the comic. Nae boring news, wurds an more wurds. No just Oor Wullie and the Broons. Ma Granny saves the comics for us. Used to bring them round tae oor auld hoose when she popped in on Mondays. Not noo. I miss her. Haven't seen her much since we came here. It's too far she says. Nae easy buses. Da gives us two brushes – one to put on the polish, one to take it off. Daft I think. Saturday nights are Cleaning Nights. Our bath nights. Aye a bath, in a bathroom. No queing fir the lavvy on the stairhead. Oh it's like they adverts for soap. But there are never bubbles for me. I'm always the last in, scudding about in my brothers' dirt. They aye come home filthy, playing in the Luggie Water or the Red Burn. When they climb in the bath Dad laughs, asks them if they like to meet some water. Oh the places we've got to play are brilliant, just like Granny promised. Miles of big green bits, trees and it isnae even a park. The grass feels brand new like nae-one's ever walked on it. Nae paths, like nae-one should walk across it. Ma brothers don't care though. They think the grass is meant for them. Say they've seen a wolf there. A big brown dug thing with a huge tail. A Super Dug. Da says it's a fox. I've heard of them. Red brown. I don't know if I want to see one though, like there on the grass, in front of me. No, I don't think so. There's nae fences round the green bits. The cars are somewhere else. And the house, a pure palace. All sparkly, everything – the paint, the floors, even the ceilings. It smells a bit funny but. Mum smiles, says it is

[3](Gaelic -Comar nan allt -the meeting of the waters)

the Fragrance of New. The house is roasty-toasty too. I love sleeping in the double room by myself until it's Mum and Da's bed-time. Then they carry me through to the settee. I don't need my own bed, I can dream anywhere. It's magic here. Nae wallpaper peeling off walls, or ice on the winter windows. You can see loads pure far away too, the sky is pure huge. At night I keek oot after Mum has drawn the blinds. Never knew there were so many stars, they make patterns in the dark. Mum loves it too, loves that it's brand new, easy to keep clean. Oh but the stairs. That's different. Nae rota, to say whose turn it is to wash them, like in the tenement. Nae card with the neighbour's names. And ootside's so messy. Folk just drap their cigarettes and chip papers, like they don't care. Mum tries. She's always down the shops for bleach. Mind you the shops are miles away. Alright if you huv a car. Nae buses, not like our old place. And they aren't proper shops. Nae corner shops open aw hours, selling ayething. They call it a Mall. I suppose it's ok when it rains. But naebody knows you, naebody remembers if you like your rolls well-fired or your sausage square or link. Mum goes up the church all the time now. She talks about taking me oan the bus tae see Granny one day. Says the church is where she meets folk. Don't know what she's talking about, there's hunners of folk here. They're no all nice though. Some of the lads an lassies bang intae you and call you names. I've stopped getting in the lift. You never know who'll get oan and where would you be then?

Finola Scott

Dawley New Town 1963-8

More of a concept than a location;
redundant Town Signs recycled into steel shutters
that lockdown the old town's High Street
bristling with barbers
glossed with nail bars
cat walked by sharp beards and models
who leave the market gazebo shelter to others.

After first plans and shelved extensions
loses its name age 5.

Captain Webb life guards the far end of the street;
his Water Fountain Monument
reminds us that nothing great comes easy
not even
losing out to Thomas Telford.

Steve Harrison

New Town, Old Story

Against a tattered backdrop curtain
of bandit machines, penny falls,

glitter ripped from the sundown town,
she careers her teary gin dance,

pinballing from bollards to chipvan,
limbs loose as ringpulls on the wind.

Some lives are hard and that is all.

Harry Gallagher

Tribes, Tech and Take Me Home – Telford is 50

I'm stuck behind a bus at traffic lights. Tapping on the steering wheel and trying to ignore the throbbing bass from the Vauxhall Corsa beside me, I stare at a big golden, sparkly 5-0. Telford hitting a half century might seem underwhelming when the town's near neighbours Shrewsbury and Stafford have Saxon roots.

Yet Telford was born, and named for a world-famous engineer, in the same year Cliff Richard's *Congratulations* topped the charts. While its neighbours register sheep and pigs and dwellings in the Domesday Book, Telford's short history might be better captured in the vivid colours of a Ladybird book or the pop art of Sergeant Pepper's.

Perhaps it's the lack of longevity – something Britons take for granted, unlike Americans – that bothers some. The belief that New Towns are manufactured and not belonging. Time has not yet allowed them to wither or, if they are showing signs of wear and tear, the chipped paint, mossy slates or cracked glass can be more accurately attributed to neglect and decay than maturity.

The charge against New Towns like Telford is that they have not grown organically, plotting their structure around medieval markets, drovers' routes, ancient highways or forgotten desire paths. Instead, critics say, town planners have rendered them sterile and uniform, fashioned from cardboard models and pencil sketches in architects' notebooks.

Yet most of us live in suburbs so I'm not sure why this makes Telford any different to the surrounding towns where swathes of identikit houses, cycle paths and roundabouts are being added to farm fields and any hint of the landscape's story – hawthorn hedge, drainage ditch or blasted oak – is scratched and burned from soil and memory. Towns are spreading and sprawling beyond ring roads and parish boundaries at such a rate the oak silhouetted against the sunset may be a lamppost or a detached garage before long.

I try to imagine a poster that might have enticed families locked in urban, post-war Brum or Wolves, or in some cases London, to the green pastures of Shropshire. Children with pageboy haircuts would lick sticky orange lollies as they ran, hand in hand down the Wrekin. Hopscotch squares would be chalked on pristine footpaths and conductors would smile and wave as buses swept along streets lined with blossoming trees.

New Towns divide people. For all the joy and skipping and Strawberry Mivvis, there is always a flipside. For some the scenes might also be captured in the Airfix modelling paint so beloved of the era, representing 1970s and 1980s Telford as a George Shaw painting, with a sense that no one really lived there, and the town was unwrapped and assembled, clipped together street by street with endless lines of streetlamps and perfectly uniform kerbs and white lines. It's hard to get away from this convenient shorthand of empty, windswept streets, the rain spattering the windowpane of our Bank Holiday childhoods.

I didn't grow up so far from Telford and when I wasn't playing I stared out at this suburban world for endless hours from the box-room of our Wimpey-built 60s semi. It was a fun, happy childhood with streams to rope-swing over and gorse and spinneys to hide in. Ice cream vans tinkled 'Popeye' and kids shinned up trees and soaked tennis balls to play cricket against garage doors. Footballs broke windows and school holidays (but never ten pence mix-ups) lasted forever.

If that all seems too saccharin and perfect, it rained endlessly too. There were three TV channels, cars broke down, tongue sandwiches existed, pet budgies died in the night. School stopped for a day when a kid in the year above got hit by a lorry. It wasn't always better, but the streets were never empty or soulless.

To celebrate the Big 5-0 Telford got on its glad rags with a laser show and a series of concerts and events for its big year. It's great to see pride in the town and I've had some great times there, playing in the town's park with my boys, trying to stay off my arse on the ice rink, or cheering on one of their favourite sons, the world middleweight champ Richie Woodhall.

New Towns haven't had the same media focus as coastal towns perhaps, but much needed investment is providing the slap to deal with some of those wrinkles. New Towns – and Telford is no exception - have suffered from some hasty construction work and infrastructure better suited to the last century. For its size Telford's rail connectivity and service should be better. There have been unwelcome headlines and there are social, economic and crime issues to resolve. This is not unique to New Towns and these issues are replicated in Stoke-on-Trent, Stafford and Wolverhampton.

It was the desire for a better life that drove Telford's population from a cluster of small towns and villages to a growing conurbation of 160,000. When New Towns were conceived cities were still coming to terms with the damage inflicted during the Second World War. People must have been delighted to get these houses and build new lives. With change there is optimism and new beginnings but also difficulty and loss. Some people in Wellington, Madeley, Oakengates and Dawley felt swallowed up and unwilling to be part of Telford.

That feeling found its way into a BBC drama *Take Me Home* where Reece Dinsdale was the London exec living in Telford and his wife played by Maggie O'Neill was increasingly isolated and despondent. Old Telford was represented by Keith Barron's taxi driver and his wife Annette Crosbie, staid and safe in their council semi-detached. The series, penned by Tony Marchant, was shot on location in Telford and dealt with Thatcherism and the shift from traditional industries to the tech sector. Settlement takes time for people and places. It wasn't a new life in Australia or Canada and may have been a move of just fifteen miles, but those that came would have left their past behind, sometimes with a heavy heart. Did they mourn families, pubs, clubs and football teams once on their doorsteps in the Black Country and Birmingham?

Identity can take generations to take root, but enjoyment of fresh air and open spaces is immediate. Short bus journeys or even walks from these new-built streets would have led their occupants to the Wrekin or Ironbridge or the farms and lanes of the Weald Moor. So, climb the Wrekin and take that steep track that turns back on itself, giving framed glimpses of the misty Shropshire plain. Step above the canopy of trees and see the silver glint of the Severn, the endless acres of reddish-brown farmland.

It is much the same landscape the Cornovii tribe, rulers of these parts, would have surveyed. For this was their hillfort. It is shrouded in cloud and stories. Is it an extinct volcano or was it created by a giant who wanted to flood Shrewsbury by tipping the mud from his shovel into the Severn? Deciding that Shrewsbury was too far away, the giant gave up, dumping the earth on the spot where he stood and forming the Wrekin.

Beneath the Wrekin the Severn twists and turns under the Ironbridge. The famous bridge is where the Industrial Revolution began, and Betjeman wrote of the first cross Channel swimmer Captain Webb 'swimming along the Severn.'

If Telford is manufactured – it was the birthplace of industry after all – it's also rooted in landscape and myth. Names remain on maps and tongues despite being swallowed by houses and bypasses. Preston-upon-the-Weald Moors, Wrockwardine, Trench and Muxton do not seem to fit in a world of granite-topped work surfaces and garden hot tubs. Similarly, a Roman super-highway, an angry giant, a forgotten tribe and a man in woollen bathers cannot be erased by town planners.

Richard Lakin

A Gap, a Construct Town, an English Edge [4]

    a cob   web a   (cr)oss   a sub   way lamp
        greasy
    moisture seeping   from bricks a skip   full
    of thoughts empty of

            selves clean gleaming

    metallic car   paint a roof   of a   build
    ing reflected   in a sh   all   ow puddle   on
    concrete pass   beneath *the* railway   to a

    sky holding a mile in its arms a gap   in a

    wire   mesh fence barbed   wire   gritty with
    rust an orange   dumper truck its   engine chu   g

    ging a trickle &   crump of its
    load dumped an   ocean   edge seep
    ing in   to scrap   metal a track to

    wards a mountainous heap of
    earth a girl   sat on *the*

    white tip   of a lock   gate's
    lever distant rain's grey

    matter   congeals to dream   a puddle half

        way a   long

Mark Goodwin

[4] after artist & retoucher Helen Suanders' *Constructed Cities & Constructed Landscapes*

In Basildon Plaza

I only understood a long time afterwards that it was pain, not rage, and that you showed your love through aggression in a moment of desolation. In the shadow of Brooke House, by the Mother and Child fountain, you wrenched at my tightly sprung corkscrews with a fine-toothed steel comb, scoured my young scalp and made me cry and then made me yelp, and then made me bleed. And I hated you hated you hated you.

Now I see. In the shadow of Brooke House, by the Mother and Child fountain, you were brushing away the loss. Brushing away the theft of your unnamed foetus. Brushing away the perfunctory incineration at the hospital *because it's for the best so you can forget – get back to normal.*

And there, in the shadow of Brooke House, by the Mother and Child fountain, we were still a family of four. Corners. Not a rounded five. A square within a square within a square. A simmering spitting meniscus at the edge of a beaten Arcadia. The necessary meta-aggression of brutalism. This plaza. Us now. Aggiornamento.

And years later. In the shadow of Brooke House, by the Mother and Child fountain, where a boy in Selassie red, green and gold had been half-drowned by skins in claret and blue, I wet my fingers and marked the V-shaped pilotis – *I hate you I hate you I hate you.*

Steve Corton

Geocaching

I am geocaching with my daughter in this new town which is four months younger than me but these bits are older than me and I am now so much older having tried to drive here using a combination of very old satnav and rather old phone and my own *OK Boomer!* stupidity, and ever since I've lived round here there have been jokes told and heard about districts and district numbers and areas like it was some dystopian television programme or never-ending series of books and confusion abounds and I wonder if it isn't the perfect place for geocaching which as far as I can tell is basically all about trying to find something or other using dodgy GPS and some weird malfunctioning equipment like my rather old phone and my very old satnav and my addled brain and if and when you find the thing you sought it's open to debate about whether or not it was truly worth it.

Rob Walton

Winter in concrete

New town with cold grey heart
decked out in facile
coloured modernity once more
but they can't change the essence
bleakness wrapped in empty
and you need to get home this winter evening
as waves of deep snow reach pale fingers
reach and grab at you stumbling
frostfeathers limn flickering traffic lights
that rattle in the snow sculpting wind
as twilight blue seeps into dark night
winter curls cold shackles
around your already chill legs
slow your way to the bus stop
to wait for transport that never comes

Kim Whysall-Hammond

THE CONTRIBUTORS

HELEN ANGELL is a poetry and non-fiction writer based in South Yorkshire, having completed an MA in Creative Writing at University of Sheffield. She has had poems published in *The Modernist, Strix, Atrium, Route 57* and *The Blue Nib* as well as an anthology published by the The Cotton Grass Appreciation Society (Maytree Press). Helen was the winner of the '*Beats Working*' Music Journalism Bursary at Sensoria Fest in 2017 and her music journalism features in *God Is In The TV* and *Dynamic* online zines. Her writing also featured in a special publication released by Penguin Random House in conjunction with Johnny Marr's '*Set The Boy Free*'.

CRAIG AUSTIN is London-based now, but retains a close link with Wales, not least in roles as Assoc. Editor of *Wales Arts Review* and as a Director of *Literature Wales*. He has been widely published in the field of the arts, and has had works of fiction published by The Lonely Press. Craig has further writing on Cwmbran due to be published in *The Modernist* magazine in a lengthy feature titled 'Rebuilding A Valley'.

JANE BURN has had her poems published in many magazines including *The Rialto, Strix, Butcher's Dog* and *Under The Radar*, and anthologies from publishers such as Seren and The Emma Press. Since 2014, her poems have had success in 43 poetry competitions. Her latest collections are *Remnants* (Knives Forks and Spoons Press, co-written with Bob Beagrie) and *Yan, Tan,Tether* (Indigo Dreams, 2020). Her poems have been nominated for the Forward and Pushcart Prize. Jane Burn is an Associate Editor at Culture Matters.

BRIAN COMBER lives in Worcestershire,England, he writes poems and short stories and has performed regularly at spoken word events in Worcester. Brian has had flash fiction published in Black Pear press anthologies, was the winner of the Worcestershire Literary Festival's '*Story on a Card*' competition in 2013 and was runner up in the 2015 National Poetry day *Light and Shade* event at Kidderminster. He has had poetry accepted for publication with Picaroon Poetry, The Beach Hut and Prole Poetry and has had poetry published in *Contour* online magazine".

STEVE CORTON Steve Corton lives in Stourbridge, West Midlands. Between the ages of 5 and 14 in the late 60s and early 70s, he lived in Stanford-Le-Hope in Essex. He was always captivated by the fountain and the tower, and would spend as long as he could on those trips sitting by the side of the water and wondering if the concrete stilts were strong enough to take the weight? Steve has only recently started submitting his written work to publishers. For the record he'd like to say: Basildon, it's not your fault. There were plenty of happy days too.

SARAH DAVY is a writer and facilitator living and working in rural Northumberland. She writes short fiction, creative non-fiction and is working on a speculative fiction novel. Sarah's work engages with the environment, people and the way they both depend on each other. She leads writing groups, workshops and retreats across Northumberland and Cumbria and loves talking about writing almost as much as writing itself.

MURDO EASON is a writer and walker based in Fife, Scotland. He is the author of *From Hill to Sea: Dispatches from the Fife Psychogeographical Collective 2010 – 2014* (Bread and Circuses Publishing, 2015) and *Language of Objects*, a collaboration with sound artist Brian Lavelle. (Blind Roads Press, 2017). Murdo grew up in the New Town of Glenrothes. He blogs at *fromhilltosea.com* and can be found on twitter @fifepsy.

HARRY GALLAGHER has 2 collections and several pamphlets to his name and has been published by Orbis,

Smokestack, Prole, Marble, IRON and many others. Harry's latest pamphlet, *English Jack*, was published in January 2020 by Black Light Engine Room Press. He runs the north east stanza of *The Poetry Society*.

MARK GOODWIN speaks and writes in various ways. He is a balancer, walker, climber, and stroller. Mark has been making poetry for over three decades, and has published six full-length books & seven chapbooks with various poetry houses. His poetry was included in *The Ground Aslant – An Anthology of Radical Landscape Poetry*, edited by Harriet Tarlo (Shearsman Books 2011) & *The Footing*, edited by Brian Lewis (Longbarrow Press, 2013). Both his books with Longbarrow – *Steps* (2014) & *Rock as Gloss* (2018) – were category finalists in the Banff Mountain Book Competition. His next book with Shearsman – *At* – is due out in spring 2020. Mark lives on a narrow-boat in Leicestershire.

STEVE HARRISON was born in Yorkshire and now lives in Shropshire where he worked teaching. His work appears in various publications from *The Emergency Poet collections, The Physic Garden, Pop Shot, Mid-Winter Solstice, HCE, Poets' Republic* to *Wetherspoons News*. He regularly performs across the Midlands and won the Ledbury Poetry Festival Slam in 2014.

SARAH JAMES is a prize-winning poet, fiction writer, journalist and photographer who fits words around life and life around words. Her latest full-length collections are *plenty-fish* (Nine Arches Press), shortlisted in the International Rubery Book Awards, and *The Magnetic Diaries* (Knives Forks and Spoons Press) highly commended in the Forward Prizes. Her website is at www.sarah-james.co.uk.

ALISON JONES is a teacher, and writer with work published in a variety of places, from Poetry Ireland Review, Proletarian Poetry and The Interpreter's House, to The Green Parent

Magazine and The Guardian. She has a particular interest in the role of nature in literature and is a champion of contemporary poetry in the secondary school classroom. Her pamphlet, *Heartwood* was published by Indigo Dreams in 2018, with a second pamphlet. *Omega*, and a full collection forthcoming in 2020.
https://www.indigodreams.co.uk/alison-jones/4594492474

RICHARD LAKIN lives in Staffordshire and writes short stories and travel pieces and occasionally poems. He has been published in numerous short story anthologies and won the Guardian family annual travel writing prize in 2013, writing about Yorkshire. In 2009 Richard won the Telegraph's *Just Back* annual prize writing about Wales.

LAURENCE MITCHELL is an established travel writer and photographer with an interest in deep topography, frontier zones and territories in transition. He has written several titles for Bradt Travel Guides (*Serbia, Kyrgyzstan, Slow Norfolk, Slow Suffolk*) as well as walking guides for Cicerone Press (*Walking in Norfolk* and *Suffolk Coast* and *Heaths Walks*). His blog *East of Elveden* features regular posts on '*hidden places, secret histories* and *unsung geography* from the east of England and beyond', which really means 'anywhere'.
https://eastofelveden.wordpress.com

HEATHER MOULSON has written poetry for four years, and has performed, and been featured at *The Poetry Cafe, Gerry's Club* and the *Slip Off Festival* in South London. Heather's pamphlet *Bunty, I miss you* is full of nostalgic smut, and a tongue in cheek hankering for a certain era. This is because 2017 Seventies was a lot more fun than the actual Seventies.

MARCELLE NEWBOLD loves poetry as a way of exploring inner digressions. She addresses the unexceptional as precious moments. A member of *The Dipping Pool* writing group, she lives in Cardiff, Wales where she trained as an architect. Twitter @marcellenewbold.

NICK PEARSON is a writer based in Wellington, Telford. Nick's poems have been widely published over the years in anthologies and magazines and he regularly performs at live literature events across the Midlands.

FINOLA SCOTT is the current Makar of The Federation of Writers (Scotland), her pamphlet, *Much left Unsaid* is published by Red Squirrel Press. Finola's poems are on posters, tapestries and postcards, in anthologies and magazines including New Writing Scotland, The Fenland Reed and Lighthouse. Her poems have won success including the Uist Prize, Dundee Competition, Coast to Coast and the Blue Nib pamphlet competitions.

BILLY STANTON is a writer and film-maker currently living in South-East London and trying to not gaze too much on the distant and enticing lights of the city. His most recent work, a short essay film about the village of Avebury, was included in the summer exhibition at the Wiltshire Museum in Devizes. He is currently working on a film about a supposed gallows-tree in the New Forest. He was born in Portsmouth, and so knows exactly what post-war re-development looks like when it both succeeds and fails.

ROB WALTON is from Scunthorpe, and now lives in Whitley Bay. His poems, flash fictions and short stories for adults and children have appeared in various anthologies and magazines in the UK, USA and New Zealand. He is currently editing his first poetry collection. His publishers include the Emma Press, Bloomsbury, Frances Lincoln, Harper Collins, IRON Press, Butcher's Dog, Smith/Doorstop, Dunlin Press, Dostoyevsky Wannabe, Strix and Arachne Press. He has also written scripts, a pathway and columns for Scunthorpe

United's matchday magazine. He sometimes tweets @anicelad.

KIM WHYSALL-HAMMOND Is a Londoner now living in Berkshire. She has been published by Total Eclipse, Ink, Sweat and Tears, Amaryllis, London Grip New Poetry and Crannóg. An expert in obsolete telecommunications arcana, Kim believes, against all evidence, that she is a good dancer. You can find her at
https://thecheesesellerswife.wordpress.com/

Printed in Great Britain
by Amazon